Edited by

**Linda Connell
& Con Connell**

D1394218

Poetry
in Stitches

National Needlework Archive

Dedications

L: For Pa.   *"At my shoulder, in my heart*
                        Though Time has past, we do not part"

C: For my father, Derrick Connell, who loved recitation, and who nurtured in me an enduring love of poetry.
        "His ready smile a parent's warmth expressed"
                                    The Deserted Village, *Oliver Goldsmith.*

Front Cover: **'Wind Farm'** *by Barbara West*
Back Cover: **'An Essay on Man'** *by Claire Fell*

First published in the United Kingdom in 2005 by
The National Needlework Archive
Boldre House, 5 Boldrewood Road
Southampton, Hampshire, SO16 7BW
Registered Charity No. 1109930
www.nationalneedleworkarchive.org.uk

Poetry in Stitches Edition © Linda Connell & Con Connell 2005
Text © Linda Connell & Con Connell
Copyright details for poems are listed on page 73
Photographs: Andy Brown, Romsey, Hampshire © NNA
Artwork: Coe and Coe, Botley, Hampshire

Printed by
Solent Design Studios
Claylands Road, Bishops Waltham
Hampshire   SO32 1BH

All Rights Reserved. No part of this publication may be reproduced or transmitted in any form or by any means, electronic or mechanical, including photocopy, recording or any other information storage and retrieval system, without prior permission in writing from the publisher.

British Library Cataloguing in Publication Data
A catalogue record for this book is available from the British Library

ISBN 0-9550790-0-4

Contents

**This publication has been made possible through the help of
generous grants from:-**

The Beatrice Trust

The Beatrice Trust was established by the family of the Editor of Poems in the Waiting Room. It has the objectives of supporting poetry, and of aiding charities caring for children with severe disabilities. The Beatrice Trust has been the principal funding source for Poems in the Waiting Room since its foundation in 1996.

and

Mrs Margaret Barraclough, in loving memory of her husband

James W Barraclough

"Happy the man, and happy he alone,
He who can call today his own:
He who, secure within, can say,
Tomorrow do thy worst, for I have lived today."
                                    Dryden

The National Needlework Archive (NNA) operates primarily to document, photograph and archive information about textile artefacts of all types and ages, which are housed in the community throughout Britain. As well as work in public buildings, offices, schools, etc., the NNA records work belonging to organisations and clubs, and facilitates the cataloguing of private collections. Additionally, the NNA maintains *The National Record of Millennium Needlework* with the associated *Stitch 2000 Research Project; the National Federation of Women's Institutes' Textile Archive*; and *The National Kneeler Database*. The NNA also promotes new work for public display, aids textile education and research, and houses books, textiles and textile related artefacts for public access.

The NNA was established in 1999 and is Registered Charity No.1109930

Poems in the Waiting Room (PitWR) is a nationwide project that provides small pamphlets of poetry for patients in health service waiting rooms. Since 1998 the poetry pamphlets have been published quarterly. Readers are invited to take the pamphlets away, and many thousands of patients have taken home a *Poems in the Waiting Room* pamphlet.

The objective of the PitWR project is to promote poetry, to make a patient's wait more pleasant, and to show appreciation for care received from the health services.
PitWR is Registered Charity No.1099033

Poetry in Stitches is a community art project launched by The National Needlework Archive in 2004 in association with Poems in the Waiting Room. The aim of the project is to combine the two important cultural media of textile art and poetry, present them in a format which allows a new perception of each in relation to the other, and to display them together in a public art arena.

Amateur and professional textile artists were invited to submit a piece of textile art inspired by a poem. The size and shape of the work was limited to 61cms (24") square, but the poem could be of their own choice.

All of the submitted textile artworks and poems were exhibited together as a collection, before being individually framed and placed in public waiting rooms or community areas for a period of between six to twelve months. The range of waiting room venues for display of the textile art pieces and poems covers health sites and similar locations across the country. As a result, thousands of people have the opportunity to study this literary and visual fusion.

This is the catalogue of the first Poetry in Stitches exhibition. All styles and textile techniques were welcomed, and the wide range employed by the artists satisfied all our hopes for diversity, covering many different types of hand and machine embroidery, quilting, tatting, rag rugs, fabric painting and feltwork. We were delighted by the variety, quality, and inspiration displayed in both the pictures and in the poems chosen. At the same time, we were delighted by the response of everyone who engaged with the vision of the project. The aim of inspiring textile artists, poets and ultimately, large groups of the general public with these artistic pairings has been so popular that we hope to continue with the project in the long term.

Anyone wishing to take part in **Poetry in Stitches**, either as a textile artist, poet, or as a host to a Poetry in Stitches picture, should see the NNA web page
www.nationalneedleworkarchive.org.uk,
or contact the NNA (*address inside front cover*) for details.

Introduction

"What a wonderful idea!"   How many times the editors heard this phrase, whilst introducing the Poetry in Stitches project to members of the embroidery, quilting, and other textile craft communities at national exhibitions.

The idea of combining visual art and poetry is not new, but the emphasis has traditionally been on *painting* and poetry.   Some poets make the link between poetry and painting explicit, for example Browning's "My Last Duchess" or Auden's "Musée des Beaux Arts", but the link is more often in one direction – the picture leads the poem – rather than the other way around.   The Poetry in Stitches project helps to redress this imbalance.

In the relationship between visual and poetic art, little attention has been given to textile art. Yet the two media complement each other by connecting with the emotional, as well as physical, senses.   Both can be intensely personal yet touch us all, in enduring ways that many other media find difficult to match.   Each medium is carefully crafted, with words or fabric painstakingly pieced together, rewarding its admirer with additional insights into the skill of the poet or artist, with each closer examination.

The textile artists who entered textile pieces for *Poetry in Stitches* were free to choose any poem as their inspiration; we offered free rein over the entire literary canon.   For those whose artistic muse required an additional nudge, we distributed a booklet of over 100 poems previously published by the *Poems in the Waiting Room* project, which were selected to encourage in our artists the awareness of a range of potential styles, rather than to restrict their choice. Some artists chose poems with strong pictorial imagery, but many preferred poems which enabled them to portray themes which struck a special chord with them, and sometimes surprised us with their subtlety.

Many traditional and well-loved pieces were chosen, including work by Blake, Byron, Herrick, Milton, Pope, Shakespeare, Shelley and Tennyson. Perhaps unsurprisingly, W.B.Yeats' "He wishes for the Cloths of Heaven" proved the most popular choice, with Edward Lear's "The Owl and the Pussycat" a close second.

A refreshing range of contemporary poets were also selected, and many of these poets wrote to say how delighted they were that their poems had been chosen. Of these twentieth century poets, some familiar poems stand out, but there are also poems not frequently anthologised, and some previously unpublished poems. Several artists chose poems that were special to them, as they were written by family members or friends.

The types of poem chosen were varied.   Many artists chose poems which had a clear narrative thread, or had strong visual cues in their text, such as 'Dream Eclipses Reality', 'The Owl and the Pussycat', or 'Warning'. Of the others, a number of the artists wrote to us sharing personal, and sometimes very moving, statements about their choice, including reminiscences of inspiring school-teachers, of encouraging parents, of memories of places as well as times, of funerals and lost friends.   Some spoke of the inspirational nature of the poem that had helped them through difficult times, either in general or at specific points in their life. Familiar themes, such as "a message of hope", were interwoven with explicit stories of pilgrimages made, and of fears overcome.   Yet some sombre tones have been leavened by laughter, with many of these personal narrative threads containing upbeat, celebratory, images; the joys of an autistic grandson, a shared family joke, the dreams of a romantic teenager. And sometimes the inspiration was simple – a poem was chosen "because it made me laugh", or "it was such a happy poem"!

As editors, we were faced with the difficult task of structuring this disparate collection in a way that would guide the reader through the artists' selection of poems and pictures. It soon became apparent that many of the poems and textile pieces reflected the essence or spirit of the four seasons; the awakenings and renewals of Spring, the energy and warmth of Summer, the visual splendour and fruitfulness of Autumn and the rawness and spirituality of Winter. Sometimes this sense resonated more in the textile, sometimes more in the poem, but this interaction highlighted the harmony of the two media working side by side. Arranging the collection in this way enabled a thread to be woven through the whole, which the reader can follow. For publishing and presentation purposes, we occasionally found it necessary to reproduce only an extract, rather than the full poem, but we have tried to keep such editing to an absolute minimum.

Our first meeting with Michael Lee, our partner at *Poems in the Waiting Room*, confirmed our belief that poets, as well as textile artists, would share our vision and be prepared to join in by allowing the NNA to place their words before textile and waiting room audiences in a textile art context. The textile artists, both professional and amateur, did not disappoint us, and this catalogue and the exhibitions it supports bear wonderful evidence to the imaginative interweaving of word and fabric.

Above all, we hope this collection of pictures and poems will enthuse the reader to continue to seek inspiration to explore their chosen medium, be it poetry or textile art.

We would like to take this opportunity to thank Michael Lee for his generous guidance and support in all manner of ways. His tireless enthusiasm for poetry and for these textile interpretations, coupled with his constant flow of good ideas, has been an inspiration to us both.

Another thank you for overwhelming support, encouragement, and proof-reading, must go to our colleague Freida Stack, whose positive approach to life lights up the week.

And last, but certainly not least, we owe a debt of great gratitude to Margaret Barraclough, an unstinting and enthusiastic supporter of the work of the National Needlework Archive from its inception, and Patron of our library.

"It's the promise of life, it's the joy in your heart."
Antonio Carlos Jobim

Spring

Springtime is a time of renewal, and this transition from a chilly, stark and bleak landscape to one of growth and regeneration is reflected in these poems. Grey skies can sometimes be transformed by rainbows, whilst underfoot the spring flowers begin to show, and the blossom signals the arrival of a fresh year.

1   **June Hurst**
Patchwork and Tambour Quilting

The Green Man

I am the face in the leaves,
I am the laughter in the forest,
I am the king in the wood.
And I am the blade of grass
That thrust through stone-cold clay
At the death of Winter.
I am before, and I am after,
I am always to the end
I am the face in the forest
I am the laughter in the leaves.

Mike Harding (1944 -   )

Millstone Quarry

There is no wind, just the chill of a grey sky.
The floor, brilliant with spring grass
is lain about with millstones: vast coins
once counted - now mossed, forgotten,

also a cattle trough. Some low earthworks
are screened by encroaching birch -
the branches crowded in a silvered frenzy.
Sheep crop silently, bleat across the stillness.

There has been recent rain. A pool mirrors
beneath the quarry face which rises,
leviathan, from the surface.
The pool collects the sky, the silence.

And later the sky gathers up into snow, falling
fragile, sinking into the stillness, the pool,
                              the waiting stone.

Isobel Campbell (1956 -   )

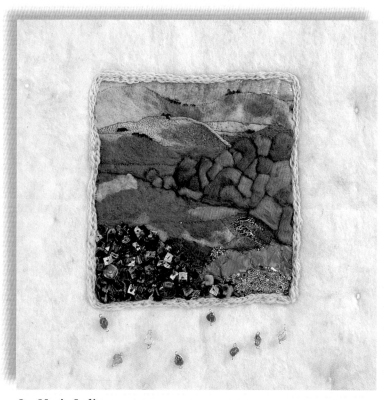

2   **Maria Lalic**
Embroidery on Hand Made Felt

Ivy

Thrown like a green shawl
Over the wall outside my kitchen window
You cling tenaciously to the red brick.
Your dark leaves greet me every day
Long after the pink blossoms of the mallow have departed
And the white flowers of the Russian Vine have blown away.
There you are still at Christmas time
Ready to be picked to decorate the table.
In Spring you hug the wall
And wait with me for the first snowdrop.

José Segal (1927 -   )

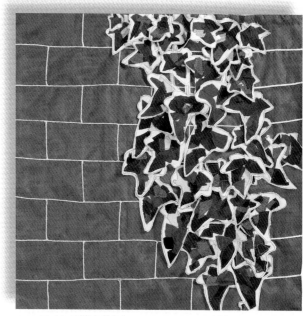

3   Linda Garstang
Applique and Free Machine Stitching

4   Clare Benson
Patchwork and Applique

5 Jackie Bowcutt
Machine Embroidery

Cherry Tree, at Dusk
for Donalda

The gales have, this past week,
been worse than at the equinox;
leaves spiralling, as though
caught in a thermal; the main bough

of next door's sycamore crazily
overhanging. Through it all, amazingly,
the blossom has clung on;
each bloom, a tiny beacon

Stewart Conn (1936 -   )

Thaw

Over the land half freckled with snow half-thawed
The speculating rooks at their nests cawed,
And saw from elm-tops, delicate as a flower of
                                                                  grass,
What we below could not see, Winter pass.

Edward Thomas (1878 - 1917)

6 Jo Baker
Patchwork and Applique

7   Donna Sales
Patchwork and Machine Quilting

Chill

Why not
let the sun in
to spread a little warmth?
It will not stay
but leave with the dusk
nor trouble your tucked-up dark.

Out-doors
it clocks the hours
on the sundial,
the seasons with flowers
wistfully while
you watch, resentfully.

But the sun
only wants to come in
to spread a little warmth
into your cold clock-watching.

J R Prynne (1938 - 2004)

Bulbs

I ask you – how the hibernating bulb
knows when to jerk awake?
Pinioned in the ice-dark earth
perpetual night of wet and cold
How does it know the time has come
to push the bleached blind maggoty shoot
out into the stone-frost dirt
on cue to flower on April 23rd?

I dare you – take a bulb and strip away
its glossy, coppery paper shell
the onion-like white folds on folds
and show me where it keeps the clock
or microchip which tells it when to start
so it will flower to the day with its companions
however chill and damp the spring.
One laggard never oversleeps and pops up in September.

I defy you - take the spiralling DNA of me
the pumping, whooshing ventricles,
the zing-charged porridge in my head,
and show me where I keep the love for you
that will outlast my life.

Maggie Butt (1955 -   )

8 Joan Brookes
Painted Fabric and Hand Embroidery

9 **Doreen E Davies**
Plain Cross Stitch

The Long-awaited Snowdrop

I waited long and looked for you to come
And now, at last, I see that you are here.
Long after you should once have long since gone
You raise your head and brave the cool crisp air.

So small and delicate in your soft, white gown,
You peep quite shyly through the melting snow.
But Ah! How bright you make my, too-long, winter.
Make keen my sense that spring comes swiftly from now on.

You will not stay for long, of that I'm certain,
But sweet and gentle presence stay a while.
Your graceful form lights up the barren garden
And draws your sisters from their winter's sleep.

D.E. Davis (1932 -)

Long awaited
Snowdrop
Clothed in White

*(Japanese inscription,
loosely translated)*

Rainbow

Did you see it, that Wednesday,
After the short, sharp shower?
A double arch, as bright as could be
Framing the apple blossom
An awesome sight to see.

No I didn't she crossly replied
I'm far too busy to look at skies!
Well, what a shame, lift up your eyes
Life's too short not to watch a rainbow

Pippa Hardy (1945 -   )

10 Lorna Morrison
Applique with Hand and Machine Embroidery

Spell to bring a smile

Come down rainbow,
Rainbow come down.

I have a space for you
in my small face

If my face is too small for you
take a space in my chest

If my chest is too small for you
take a space in my belly

If my belly is too small for you
then take every part of me

Come down Rainbow
Rainbow come down

You can eat me from head to toe.

John Agard (1949 -   )

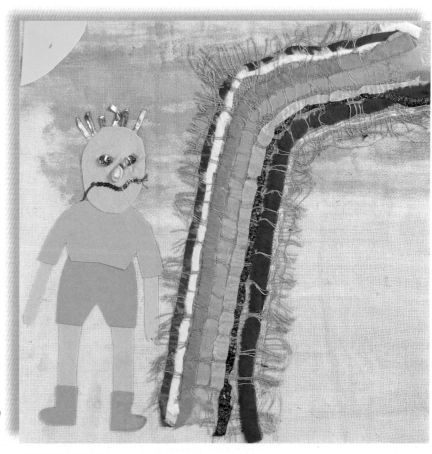

11 Aidan Tulloch (age 5 years)
Woven Ribbon on Painted Fabric, Applied Figure

Sound of Song

Colours of the rainbow
Dancing in the dark
Gentle sliding little lights
Flowing into sparks

If you could see the sound of song
A storm of coloured light
Twisting, twirling, pulsing
Dancing notes in flight

A rainbow on wings
Heartfelt feelings,
Living notes
Your own unique kaleidoscope

Dawn Ashcroft (1947 -)

12 Dawn Ashcroft
Machine Embroidery with some Hand Stitching

13 Linda Ellis
Canvas Work

***Dream
Eclipses
Reality***

14 Carol Baker
Applique

Dream Eclipses Reality

Yesterday I painted
Great big happy faces
On all the skyscrapers
In the Gorbals...
And what if skyscrapers
Really did scrape
The sky?
I would attach paintbrushes
Dripping with rainbow colours
To their radio masts
And lightning conductors.

Dee Rimbaud (1962 -   )

15 Karin Keddy
Hand and Machine Embroidery on Paper

16 Delia Garrod
Applique with Hand Embroidery

Empty

Empty
The tomb empty
Life is like that tomb
Empty
Without Jesus

Delia Garrod (1947 -   )

17 Marlene Cohen
Patchwork.   Machine Quilting

Red Gleam

Red gleam,
Dark needlepoint
Through to the clarion-call
Of extremes.
Here. Now.
Advent necessity
Of the new century
Spring-piercing the forge
Of the earth's wounds
Into new frequencies.

Long arm of ancient strand
Pointing the same story,
The one we know,
This is where we are
Where we tumble down
Storm-ridden deserts
And watery depths
Into higher and higher
Firmaments.

Required of us...
Dispersal of minutiae
To the wider stream
As new stars unfold horizons
Not yet dreamed of,
And the pioneer's keen
Reaches beyond even
Our rarest intention.
How, how may we dare
The clarity required,
God hold us, hold us all.

Prue Fitzgerald

A Slash of Blue

A slash of Blue -
A sweep of Gray -
Some scarlet patches on the way,
Compose an Evening Sky -
A little purple - slipped between -
Some Ruby Trousers hurried on -
A Wave of Gold -
A Bank of Day -
This just makes out the Morning Sky.

Emily Dickinson (1830 – 1886)

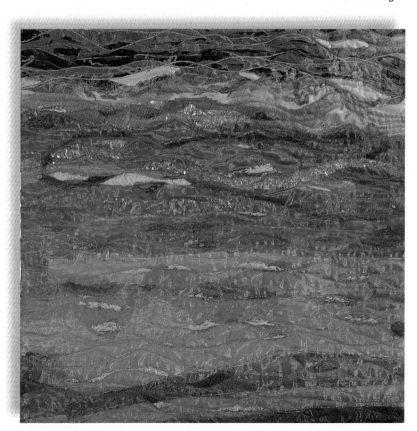

18 Dorothy Balfour
Layered Fabrics, Bonded, Cut, and Stitched

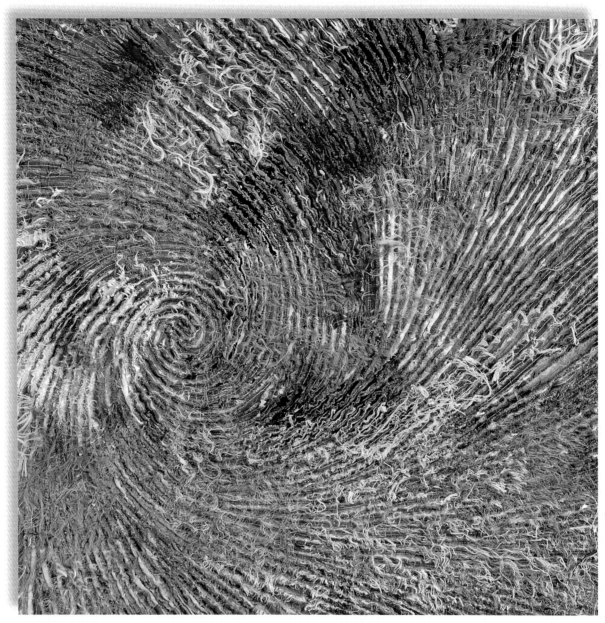

19 Carol Dale
Chenille. Slashed layers of fabric with Machine Stitching

Waters of March (extract)

A stick, a stone,
It's the end of a road,
It's the rest of a stump,
It's a little alone

It's a sliver of glass,
It is light, it's the sun,
It is night, it is death,
It's a trap, it's a gun

The oak when it blooms,
A fox in the brush,
A knot in the wood,
The song of a thrush

The wood of the wind,
A cliff, a fall,
A scratch, a lump,
It is nothing at all.

It's the wind blowing free,
It's the end of the slope,
It's a beam, it's a void,
It's a hunch, it's a hope.

A fish, a flash,
A silvery glow,
A fight, a bet,
The range of a bow

Afloat, adrift,
A flight, a wing,
A hawk, a quail,
The promise of Spring

And the river bank talks
Of the waters of March
It's the promise of life,
It's the joy in your heart.

Antonio Carlos Jobim (1927 – 1994)

Learn to make the best of Life

Learn to make the best of life
Lose no golden day.
Time will never bring you back
Chances swept away.
Leave no tender word unsaid
Love while love may last.
The mill will never grind with
Water that is past.

Anon

20 Hilary Sugai
Machine Embroidery with Hand-worked Embellishment

21 Vera Baker
Rug Hooking

Thank you

Thank you for
The trees and flowers,
The good green grass
And sunny hours.

For spiders' webs
All bright with dew,
And leafy chinks
For peeping through.

For all the good things
Growing wild
That make life happy
For a child.

Kathleen Partridge

Partings

Whenever you say goodbye
Do seek each other out,
Don't hurry through the back door
With just a goodbye shout.

Maybe you hug each other
Or wave at the front door
It might be a farewell kiss
Or even two or more.

Make peace if necessary
Don't criticise or moan
You both have faults, remember
Before you're left alone.

Sometime it could even be
The last goodbye you'll say
And then you can't help thinking
Just how you went your way.

Because all life's uncertain
That last time means a lot
It brings a quirky smile
When mem'ry's all you've got.

Don't part though with foreboding
Nor yet a sense of fear
But loving recognition
Of someone you hold dear.

All this could be old-fashioned
With mobile phones to play
Still. Make the parting special
With your best friend today.

I. K Leavers (1920 - 2002)

22 Sharon Frogley
Applique with Machine Stitching

17

Naming of Parts

To-day we have naming of parts. Yesterday,
We had daily cleaning. And to-morrow morning,
We shall have what to do after firing. But to-day,
To-day we have naming of parts. Japonica
Glistens like coral in all of the neighbouring gardens,
          And to-day we have naming of parts.

This is the lower sling swivel. And this
Is the upper sling swivel, whose use you will see,
When you are given your slings. And this is the piling swivel,
Which in your case you have not got. The branches
Hold in the gardens their silent, eloquent gestures,
          Which in our case we have not got.

This is the safety-catch, which is always released
With an easy flick of the thumb. And please do not let me
See anyone using his finger. You can do it quite easy
If you have any strength in your thumb. The blossoms
Are fragile and motionless, never letting anyone see
          Any of them using their finger.

And this you can see is the bolt. The purpose of this
Is to open the breech, as you see. We can slide it
Rapidly backwards and forwards: we call this
Easing the spring. And rapidly backwards and forwards
The early bees are assaulting and fumbling the flowers
          They call it easing the Spring.

They call it easing the Spring: it is perfectly easy
If you have any strength in your thumb: like the bolt,
And the breech, and the cocking-piece, and the point of balance,
Which in our case we have not got; and the almond-blossom
Silent in all of the gardens and the bees going backwards and forwards,
          For to-day we have naming of parts.

Henry Reed (1914 - 1986)

23 Margaret Fowkes
Mixed Lacework Techniques

24 Jill Findlay
Applique with Hand and Machine Stitching

Mrs Southern's Enemy (extract)

Dear Mrs Southern ....
In a wide blue skirt, white spotted, and white apron;
On the very top of her head she carried a cap,
An emblem of respect and respectability, while
As though she were a Hindu charmer of snakes,
Her hair lay coiled and tame at the back of her head.
But her actual majesty was really the golden glory
Through which she moved, a hurrying fly
Enshrined in a rolling amber;
As she spun along in a twisting column of golden atoms,
A column of gold motes above and around her,
A column of visible, virtuous activity.

She did not recognise her enemy.
She thought him Dust:
But what is Dust
Save Time's most lethal weapon ....

Osbert Sitwell (1892-1969)

19

25 Christine Hepburn
Patchwork with Hand and Machine Quilting

Footprints

One night a man had a dream. He dreamed
he was walking along the beach with the LORD.
Across the sky flashed scenes from his life.
For each scene he noticed two sets of
footprints in the sand: one belonging
to him, and the other to the LORD.

When the last scene of his life flashed before him,
he looked back at the footprints in the sand.
He noticed that many times along the path of
his life there was only one set of footprints.
He also noticed that it happened at the very
lowest and saddest times in his life.

This really bothered him and he
questioned the LORD about it:
"LORD, you said that once I decided to follow you,
you'd walk with me all the way.
But I have noticed that during the most
troublesome times in my life,
there is only one set of footprints.
I don't understand why, when
I needed you most, you would leave me."

The LORD replied:
"My son, my precious child,
I love you and I would never leave you.
During your times of trial and suffering,
when you see only one set of footprints,
it was then that I carried you."

Anon

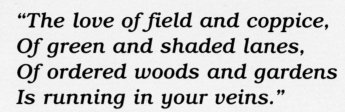

*"The love of field and coppice,
Of green and shaded lanes,
Of ordered woods and gardens
Is running in your veins."*

Dorothea McKellar

Summer

Sandy beaches, gardens in bloom and cricket on the village green are quintessential images of a traditional British summer. The sunny images of verdant rural fields and dry city centres are complemented by tales of the sea and impressions of warm, moonlit evenings or dreams of faraway places.

26 **Marilyn Jones**
Painted Fabric. Hand and Machine Embroidery

Questions in Eden

For my delight are butterflies.
Warm scarf of sun about my
neck, a wind,
just mildly frivolous with stems,
teases the flowers. So delectable,
my little world of bees and balm.

Who decided on rose-purple for these asters
then tossed handfuls of butterflies to
      bounce and land
on every buzzing sweet of marigold?
Why do I mourn for peacock wings ensnared
in spider's gossamer, yet give to
      burnished beetle
freedom to clockwork away at aphids
      for his lunch?

Why must I take sides? Does anything
even need a reason to be –
if all's so madly – oh so maddeningly –
Beautiful?

Joan Kingston (1920 -)

Adlestrop

Yes, I remember Adlestrop -
The name, because one afternoon
Of heat the express-train drew up there
Unwontedly. It was late June.

The steam hissed. Someone cleared
     his throat.
No one left and no one came
On the bare platform. What I saw
Was Adlestrop - only the name

And willows, willow-herb, and grass,
And meadowsweet, and haycocks dry,
No whit less still and lonely fair
Than the high cloudlets in the sky.

And for that minute a blackbird sang
Close by, and round him, mistier,
Farther and farther, all the birds
Of Oxfordshire and Gloucestershire.

Edward Thomas (1878 – 1917)

27 **Eileen Robinson**
Painted Fabric. Applique and Machine Stitching

28 Judy Fairless
Applique with Machine Quilting

Fast Bowler

The feel of ball in hand
the bite of seam on fingers
the snug, tight-but-loose grip of it.

The batsman waits
bat anxiously tapping, tapping
You set your will against his

begin to run
slowly at first
Accelerating
feet barely stroking the ground
then burst
into that explosive leap,
fingers working the seam.

The ball arcs
like blood on snow,
deceives
then strikes like a snake from the grass.

And, oh, if all is right
you know there will be
such a riot of wood
such catherine wheels of timber
such sparkling, tumbling varnish
that you will hug it to your heart
and feel the glow
throughout the long, back-aching
wicketless afternoon.

Tony Turner (1933 -   )

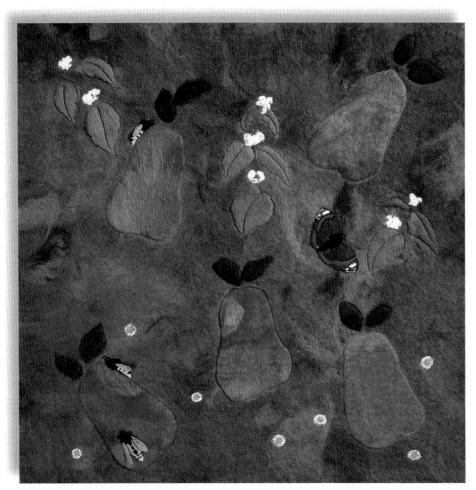

29 **Ailsa Bulger**
Felt with Machine and Hand Stitching

I would not have you perfect

I would not have you perfect
an Adam before the Fall
tending a perfect garden
a paradise of sound and scent
the home of brilliant birds.

I would have you as you are,
the daisied lawn unmown,
nettles seducing butterflies,
pears fermenting where they fall,
wasps drunk in a rotting Eden.

I would not have you perfect
like Sunday china under glass.
I would have you earthenware,
crazed chipped for everyday,
bought on the market stall.

I would not have you perfect.
I would have you as you are
like a tarnished looking glass
not one unblemished where I see
reflected all my flaws.

Joan Goodall *(1928 -)*

Circle Poem

Alec Finlay (1966 -)

30 **Penny Godfrey**
Rag Rug Hooking

31 Sally Kelly
Applique with Surface Stitching

Streetwonders

Small fortitudes may sometimes
mend holes in a day, help make it
seem golden. Those who do this may
                                    pick out
lost music in some small street noise
or may see the dance of summer shadows
over last year's fallen leaves.
On such a day we find
lost keys, and missing friends
appear.

Peter Williamson (1913 -   )

Sanctuary

I have a place where I may go,
And keep myself apart;
Sometimes a room within a house
Sometimes within the heart,

Of a long bramble by a wall
Pink-petaled in the clod;
And there I steep in loveliness,
And hear god call to god.

For loveliness is not in bulk;
A rose may harbour me, -
(A thing in need of lovely things) –
Or a tower by the sea.

Lizette Woodworth Reese (1856 – 1935)

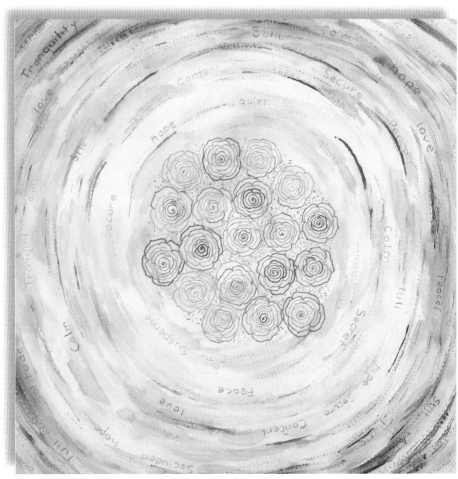

32 Janet Hunter
Painted Fabric. Hand Embroidery

33 Gisburn Road Community Primary School Sewing Club
Fabric Collage. Hand Embroidery

The Quangle Wangle's Hat

On the top of the Crumpetty Tree
   The Quangle Wangle sat,
But his face you could not see,
   On account of his Beaver Hat.
For his hat was a hundred and two feet wide,
With ribbons and bibbons on every side
And bells, and buttons, and loops, and lace,
So that nobody ever could see the face
   Of the Quangle Wangle Quee.

The Quangle Wangle said
   To himself on the Crumpetty Tree,
'Jam; and jelly; and bread;
   'Are the best food for me!
'But the longer I live on this Crumpetty Tree
'The plainer than ever it seems to me
'That very few people come this way
'And that life on the whole is far from gay!'
   Said the Quangle Wangle Quee.

But there came to the Crumpetty Tree,
   Mr. and Mrs. Canary;
And they said,—'Did you ever see
   'Any spot so charmingly airy?
'May we build a nest on your lovely Hat?
Mr. Quangle Wangle, grant us that!
'O please let us come and build a nest
'Of whatever material suits you best,
   'Mr. Quangle Wangle Quee!'

And besides, to the Crumpetty Tree
   Came the Stork, the Duck, and the Owl;
The Snail, and the Bumble-Bee,
The Frog, and the Fimble Fowl;
(The Fimble Fowl, with a Corkscrew leg;)
And all of them said,—We humbly beg,
'We may build our homes on your lovely Hat,
'Mr. Quangle Wangle, grant us that!
   'Mr. Quangle Wangle Quee!'

And the Golden Grouse came there,
   And the Pobble who has no toes,
And the small Olympian bear,
And the Dong with a luminous nose.
And the Blue Babboon, who played the flute,
And the Orient Calf from the Land of Tute,
And the Attery Squash, and the Bisky Bat,
All came and built on the lovely Hat
   Of the Quangle Wangle Quee.

And the Quangle Wangle said
To himself on the Crumpetty Tree,
'When all these creatures move
'What a wonderful noise there'll be!'
And at night by the light of the Mulberry moon
They danced to the flute of the Blue Babboon,
On the broad green leaves of the Crumpetty Tree,
And all were as happy as happy could be,
   With the Quangle Wangle Quee.

Edward Lear (1812 – 1888)

The Swing

How do you like to go up in a swing,
Up in the air so blue?
Oh, I do think it the pleasantest thing
Ever a child can do!

Up in the air and over the wall,
Till I can see so wide,
Rivers and trees and cattle and all
Over the countryside

Till I look down on the garden green,
Down on the roof so brown -
Up in the air I go flying again,
Up in the air and down!

Robert Louis Stevenson (1850 -1894)

34 Isabel McInnes
Stumpwork Figure. Hand and Machine Embroidery

Traditional Prize County Pigs: Staffordshire Tamworth Red

If you want to go away
On a sunny holiday
And take your pig, make no mistake
A Tamworth Red's the pig to take.

A pig whose skin is very fair
Will use up all your Ambre Solaire,
And need a hat, and cause concern,
But Tamworths very seldom burn.

Wendy Cope (1945 -   )

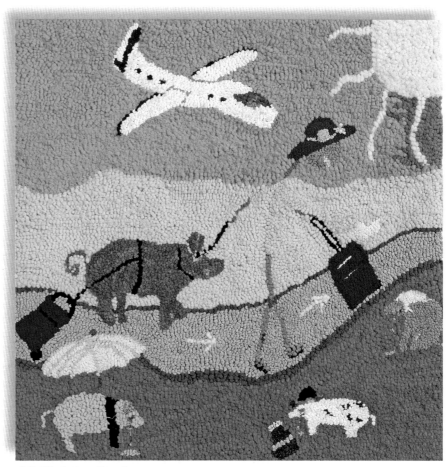

35 Christine Steele
Rag Rug Hooking

The Voyage with the Nautilus (extract)

I made myself a little boat
As trim as trim could be;
I made it of a great pearl shell
Found in the Indian Sea.

I made my masts of wild sea-rush
That grew on a secret shore,
And the scarlet plume of the halcyon
Was the pleasant flag I bore.

For my sails I took the butterfly's wings;
For my ropes the spider's line;
And that mariner old, the Nautilus,
To steer me over the brine.

"Now steer away, thou helmsman good,
Over the waters free;
To the charmed Isle of the Seven Kings,
That lies in the midmost sea."

He turned the helm; away we sailed
Towards the setting sun;
The flying fish were swift of wing,
But we outsped each one.

Down and down went the setting sun,
And down and down went we;
'Twas a splendid sail for several days
On a smooth descending sea.

So on we went; but soon I heard
A sound as when winds blow,
And waters wild are tumbled down
Into a gulf below.

And on and on flew the little bark,
As a fiend her course did urge;
And I saw in a moment we must hang
Upon the ocean's verge.

And for thrice seven days we sailed and sailed;
At length I saw the bay
Where I built my ship, and my mother's house
'Mid the green hills where it lay.

"Farewell!" said I to the Nautilus,
And leaped upon the shore;
"Thou art a skilful mariner,
But I'll sail with thee no more!"

Mary Howitt (1799-1888)

36 Christine Pulker
Collage. Machine Embroidery

37 Anne-Marie Stewart
Machine Quilting

After Dark at Yachtsman's Cottage

Open the window
To the night
And soft murmurings
Of dark water
Bubbling with curlews
And the muted
Barking of dogs
From moored barges.
Now distant lights
Red, yellow, green,
As a heartbeat
Sails slowly seawards
And I wait
Until its waves
Like rippling applause
Reach the shore

Richard Stewart (1945 -)

Sea Fever

I must down to the seas again,
      to the lonely sea and the sky,
And all I ask is a tall ship
      and a star to steer her by,
And the wheel's kick and the wind's song
      and the white sail's shaking,
And a grey mist on the sea's face,
      and a grey dawn breaking.

I must down to the seas again,
      for the call of the running tide
Is a wild call and a clear call
      that may not be denied;
And all I ask is a windy day
      with the white clouds flying,
And the flung spray and the blown spume,
      and the sea-gulls crying.

I must down to the seas again,
      to the vagrant gypsy life,
To the gull's way and the whale's way
      where the wind's like a whetted knife;
And all I ask is a merry yarn
      from a laughing fellow-rover
And quiet sleep and a sweet dream
      when the long trick's over.

John Masefield (1878 – 1967)

38 Betty Sneap
Patchwork with Hand Quilting. Bead Embellishment

So we'll go no more a-roving

So, we'll go no more a-roving
  So late into the night,
Though the heart be still as loving,
  And the moon be still as bright.
For the sword outwears its sheath,
  And the soul wears out the breast,
And the heart must pause to breathe,
  And love itself have rest.
Though the night was made for
                           loving,
  And the day returns too soon,
Yet we'll go no more a-roving
  By the light of the moon.

Lord Byron (1788 – 1824)

39 Vivien Stamford
Machine and Hand Embroidery

She Walks in Beauty

40 Wendy Scattergood
Mixed Media. Applique. Hand and Machine Stitching

41 Hilary Burton
Patchwork and Applique. Hand Quilting

She Walks in Beauty

She walks in beauty like the night
Of cloudless climes and starry skies,
And all that's best of dark and bright
Meet in her aspect and her eyes;
Thus mellowed to the tender light
Which heaven to gaudy day denies.

One ray the more, one shade the less
Had half impaired the nameless grace
Which waves in every raven tress

Or softly lightens o'er her face,
Where thoughts serenely sweet express
How pure, how dear their dwelling place.

And on that cheek and o'er that brow
So soft, so calm yet eloquent,
The smiles that win, the tints that glow
But tell of days in goodness spent
A mind at peace with all below,
A heart whose love is innocent.

Lord Byron (1788 – 1824)

Petra (extract)

It seems no work of Man's creative hand,
By labour wrought as wavering fancy planned;
But from the rock as by magic grown,
Eternal, silent, beautiful, alone!
Not virgin-white like that old Doric shrine,
Where erst Athena held her rites divine;
Not saintly-grey, like many a minster fane,
That crowns the hill and consecrates the plain;
But rose-red as if the blush of dawn,
That first beheld them were not yet withdrawn;
The hues of youth upon a brow of woe,
Which Man deemed old two thousand years ago.
Match me such marvel save in Eastern clime,
A rose-red city half as old as time.

John William Burgon (1813 -1888)

42 Doreen Healey
Patchwork. Hand and Machine Stitching

43 Margaret Ramsay
Image Transfer. Patchwork and Machine Quilting

44 Jenny Longhurst
Applique and Layering. Hand and Machine Stitching

My Country

The love of field and coppice,
Of green and shaded lanes,
Of ordered woods and gardens
Is running in your veins.
Strong love of grey-blue distance,
Brown streams and soft, dim skies –
I know but cannot share it,
My love is otherwise.

I love a sunburnt country,
A land of sweeping plains,
Of ragged mountain ranges,
Of droughts and flooding rains.
I love her far horizons,
I love her jewel-sea,
Her beauty and her terror –
The wide brown land for me!

The stark white ring-barked forests,
All tragic to the moon,
The sapphire-misted mountains,
The hot gold hush of noon,
Green tangle of the brushes
Where lithe lianas coil,
And orchids deck the tree-tops,
And ferns the warm dark soil.

Core of my heart, my country!
Her pitiless blue sky,
When, sick at heart, around us
We see the cattle die –
But then the grey clouds gather,
And we can bless again
The drumming of an army,
The steady soaking rain.

Core of my heart, my country!
Land of the rainbow gold,
For flood and fire and famine
She pays us back threefold.
Over the thirsty paddocks,
Watch, after many days,
The filmy veil of greenness
That thickens as we gaze.

An opal-hearted country,
A wilful, lavish land –
All you who have not loved her,
You will not understand –
Though earth holds many splendours,
Wherever I may die,
I know to what brown country
My homing thoughts will fly.

Dorothea McKellar (1885 – 1968)

33

45 Evelyn Bernardi
Painted Fabric with Applique and Hand Embroidery

To a Skylark (extract)

Hail to thee, blithe spirit!
Bird thou never wert,
That from heaven, or near it
Pourest thy full heart
In profuse strains of
        unpremeditated art.

Higher still and higher
From the earth thou springest
Like a cloud of fire;
The blue deep thou wingest,
And singing still dost soar,
        and soaring ever singest.

In the golden lightning
Of the sunken sun,
O'er which clouds are bright'ning,
Thou dost float and run;
Like an unbodied joy whose
        race is just begun.

Percy Bysshe Shelley (1792 – 1822)

Redstart in a Welsh Wood

Lichen drips green light
Under trees that grapple together;
Moss muffles dark knuckles of cragside.
Young ferns are wafted by currents
In the underwater gloom
Where grey cobwebs float from bark.

Then suddenly you are there,
Glowing with the sun of Africa,
Trailing behind you shimmering fires.
Nervous and trembling
You sprinkle the glades with
        flickering light,
Your tail aflame in its own heat haze;
As you drop to the ground
It touches Welsh grindstone
And sparks fly.
Then up again on a quivering branch
To powder the leaves with fiery dust.
Where you are it is sunlight.

But now the sunlight is gone.
Bare trees tie hillsides
In tight knots.
Lichen weeps black tears
And the wood waits for
        the Redstart's return

Mike Mockler

46 Penny Martin
Burning and Free Embroidery

Hawk in the Grey Morning

You hang in the grey mistiness,
Glimpsed at a distance, yet
It is as if I can feel
The vibration of your wings,
Warmth of your back,
Taut muscles underlying the humming flight feathers,
And the dampness of your mist-speckled plumage.
I celebrate, without understanding,
The connection we have,
And long to touch your damp, pulsating warmth,
Hold you, cupped in my hands
Gently.

Mollie Mayson (1939 -   )

47 Patricia McLaughlin
Hand Applique. Machine Quilting

48 Penny Dickson
Image Transfer. Patchwork. Machine Quilting

The Other Side of the Valley

The sun has come out late today
and lights the golden fields,
making them look nearer now.
The hay is waiting to be gathered,
rolled up in neat carpets,
soaking the last warmth of pale sunlight.

I would like to go to the hills,
(too far; too late)
Watch the shadows from the hedges
close in until there is nothing left
but one small wedge of light,
that you can hold in your hand
and throw up into the darkening sky
to burst into a million tiny stars.

Idris Caffrey (1949 -   )

49 Ann Collard
Painted Fabric with Applique and Embroidery

New Every Morning

Every day is a fresh beginning,
Listen my soul to the glad refrain.
And, spite of old sorrows
And older sinning,
Troubles forecasted
And possible pain,
Take heart with the day and
              begin again.

Susan Coolidge (1835-1905)

50 Judith Anderson
Applique with Machine Embroidery.

Nocturne

Sometimes the moon deceives
Turning shadows into phantoms
But usually things are
As they are.

The young, restless water
Gushes over ancient millstones
And saplings close canopied
Ache for the sun's burning light.

Richard Stewart (1945 -   )

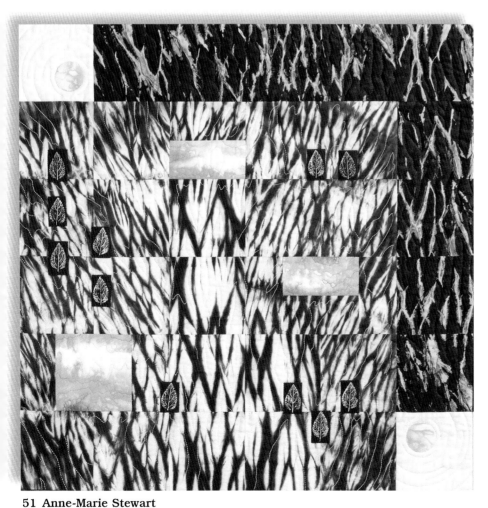

51 Anne-Marie Stewart
Patchwork with Machine Quilting

52 Barbara Deason
Hand Embroidery

The Gate of the Year

I said to the man who stood at the gate
    of the year
'Give me a light that I may tread safely
    into the unknown.'

And he replied, 'Go into the darkness
    and put your hand into the hand of God
That shall be to you better than light
    and safer than a known way!'

So I went forth and finding the Hand of God
Trod gladly into the night
He led me towards the hills
And the breaking of day in the lone east.

So heart be still!
What need our human life to know
If God hath comprehension?

In all the dizzy strife of things
Both high and low,
God hideth his intention.

Minnie Louise Haskins (1875 – 1957)

"The trees are undressing, and fling in many places –
On the gray road, the roof, the window-sill –
Their radiant robes and ribbons and yellow laces;"

Thomas Hardy

Autumn

Deep reds and golds of late autumnal evenings are a
feature of many of these poems. Metaphors of needle and
thread, as well as stitching itself, feature strongly as the
days get shorter. Some late-summer whimsy is tempered
by October's Charge of the Light Brigade.

Wild Geese

You do not have to be good.
You do not have to walk on your knees
for a hundred miles through the desert repenting.
You only have to let the soft animal of your body
love what it loves.

Tell me about despair, yours, and I will tell you mine.
Meanwhile the world goes on.
Meanwhile the sun and the clear pebbles of the rain
are moving across the landscapes,
over the prairies and the deep trees,
the mountains and the rivers.
Meanwhile the wild geese, high in the clean blue air,
are heading home again.

Whoever you are, no matter how lonely,
the world offers itself to your imagination,
calls to you like the wild geese, harsh and exciting –
over and over announcing your place
in the family of things.

Mary Oliver (1935 -)

53 Nikki Tinkler
Patchwork. Machine Quilting

54 Kate Dowty
Patchwork and Layering. Hand and Machine Quilting

Sunset

Evening slowly spreads a new cloth,
held by a frame of olden trees.
You watch. Two separate worlds slip away;
one rises to heaven: one falls to earth

and leaving you, belonging wholly to neither,
not so dark as the silent house;
not so clear as the eternity
which becomes a star, rising each night,

and leaving you – unable to untangle the threads –
your life; timid and eager and fruitful
as it is: sometimes held down; sometimes exultant;
moment to moment – now stone, now star.

Rainer Maria Rilke (1875 – 1926)
(trans. Michael Lee 2004)

55 Mimi Beckett (age 13 years)
Patchwork and Applique

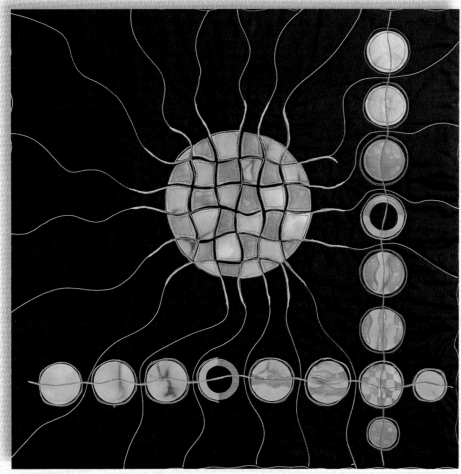

56 Sara Cook
Applique and Machine Quilting

Planetary Alignment

Astrologically speaking,
All the signs look promising.
But she's still not sure
Who should be entering
                    whose house.

Affairs of the heart
Are still just affairs.
Eclipses still depend on
Where you're standing.
Mars and Venus still keep
                    their distance,
Only appearing to touch.

Con Connell (1949 -   )

Stitched together over time (extract)

Like an old patchwork quilt – multicoloured,
A messy assortment of mismatching fabrics
Stitched together over time – the story of my life
Is recorded upon the landscape of my mind.
Creases here and there obstruct the view.
Years are blocked out, or exist only as a blur:
A faded snapshot here; a thirty second mpeg there -
Distorted, out of focus, mere flickers of information
Incomprehensible as any kind of linear whole.
Yet nothing is lost: every memory, moment, event –
Be it brilliant, shiny and new; or dull, almost forgotten
                                        – is there,
Sewn securely into the network of the weave.

Rebecca Atherton (1977 -   )

57 Janet Atherton
Photo Transfer with Hand Embroidery

58 Yvonne Blatchford
Patchwork with Machine Quilting

The last week in October

The trees are undressing, and fling in many places –
On the gray road, the roof, the window-sill –
Their radiant robes and ribbons and yellow laces;
A leaf each second is so flung at will,
Here, there, another and another, still and still.

A spider's web has caught one while downcoming,
That stays there dangling when the rest pass on;
Like a suspended criminal hangs he, murmuring
In golden garb, while one yet green, high yon,
Trembles, as fearing such a fate for himself anon.

Thomas Hardy (1840 – 1928)

Marigolds

You've watched them for months,
counted the tiny pincushion heads,
and if you, somehow, missed
          the unpicking
of the tight green binding, you saw
fringe after fringe of petals
loosen morning by morning.
You watered them, from the base
like you knew you should,
blew away traffic dust
from their burnt knot faces,
narrowing your nostrils
against the smell.
Later, you pinched finger
 and thumb
round the hollow stem
of a fraying head
and twisted. Let it drop
to the flags, unseeded,
to be trampled
till it streaked the stone
like butterfly wings.
All this, you've done since June.
It's October now.
They're still going strong,
golden and sour.

Helen Clare (1965 -   )

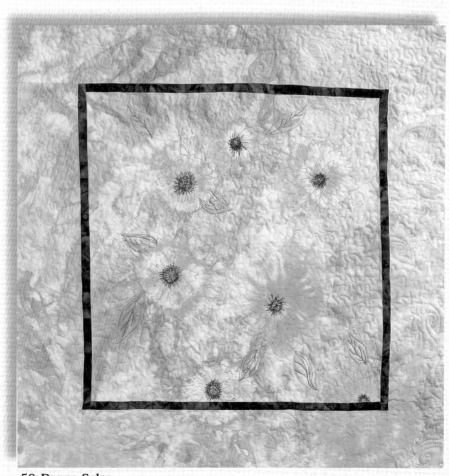

59 Donna Sales
Machine Quilting

60 Cardiff Picot and ISCA Tatters
Tatting

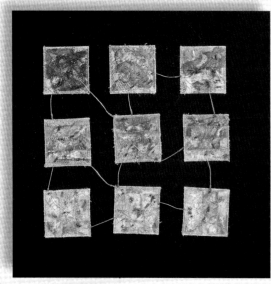

61 Beverley Folkard
Embellished Applique with Machine Embroidery

Warning

When I am an old woman I shall wear purple
With a red hat which doesn't go, and doesn't suit me.
And I shall spend my pension on brandy and summer gloves
And satin sandals, and say we've no money for butter.
I shall sit down on the pavement when I'm tired
And gobble up samples in shops and press alarm bells
And run my stick along the public railings
And make up for the sobriety of my youth.
I shall go out in my slippers in the rain
And pick the flowers in other people's gardens
And learn to spit.

You can wear terrible shirts and grow more fat
And eat three pounds of sausages at a go
Or only bread and pickle for a week
And hoard pens and pencils and beermats and things in boxes.

But now we must have clothes that keep us dry
And pay our rent and not swear in the street
And set a good example for the children.
We must have friends to dinner and read the papers.

But maybe I ought to practice a little now?
So people who know me are not too shocked and surprised
When suddenly I am old, and start to wear purple.

Jenny Joseph (1932 -   )

62 Elizabeth Smith
Applique and Machine Embroidery

Just One More

You can't ever have enough fabric
Even if you have bags of the stuff!
If you bought only, say,
One fat quarter a day
That wouldn't be nearly enough!

You can't ever have enough fabric
Even if you have boxfuls at home!
For waiting somewhere
Is that one special square
'Though you've combed every shop you can comb!

You can't ever have enough fabric
Even if you have chestfuls by now!
You can squeeze one piece more
In that very full drawer.
It will all come in someday, somehow!

You can't ever have too much fabric,
Like you can't ever have too much air!
So you'll add "just one more"
To that much-treasured store
And you know you can use it somewhere!

So at last, when the one Great Quilter
Calls you home to Her workroom above,
And your every block fits
And you make your last stitch
And you lay down your labour of love

Then remember that She shares your passions
Because She can't resist "just one more".
She'll somehow find space
For just one more place
As She gathers you into Her store.

Con Connell (1949 -   )

63 Linda Connell
Applique and Machine Quilting

The Owl and the Pussycat

64 Frances McArthur
Patchwork and Applique.   Machine Quilting

The Owl and the Pussy-cat went to sea
In a beautiful pea green boat,
They took some honey, and plenty of money,
Wrapped up in a five pound note.

The Owl looked up to the stars above,
And sang to a small guitar,
'O lovely Pussy! O Pussy my love,
What a beautiful Pussy you are,
You are,
You are!
What a beautiful Pussy you are!'

65 Isabel Hewitt
Patchwork and Applique. Hand Quilting

Pussy said to the Owl, 'You elegant fowl!
How charmingly sweet you sing!
O let us be married! too long we have tarried:
But what shall we do for a ring?'

66 Jennifer Hills
Patchwork and Applique. Machine Quilting

They sailed away, for a year and a day,
To the land where the Bong-tree grows
And there in a wood a Piggy-wig stood
With a ring at the end of his nose,
His nose,
His nose,
With a ring at the end of his nose.

Dear Pig, are you willing to sell for one shilling
Your ring?' Said the Piggy, 'I will.'
So they took it away, and were married next day
By the Turkey who lives on the hill.

67 Westbury-on-Trym Tatters
Tatting on Felt

They dined on mince, and slices of quince,
Which they ate with a runcible spoon;
And hand in hand, on the edge of the sand,
They danced by the light of the moon,
The moon,
The moon,
They danced by the light of the moon.

Edward Lear (1812 – 1888)

68 Ring of Tatters, Essex Branch
Tatting

69 April Twigg
Patchwork. Layering. Machine Top Stitching and Quilting

70 Sue Dove
Patchwork with Hand Embroidery

He Wishes For
the Cloths of Heaven

Had I the heavens' embroidered cloths,
Enwrought with golden and silver light,
The blue and the dim and the dark cloths
Of night and light and the half-light,
I would spread the cloths under your feet:
But I, being poor, have only my dreams;
I have spread my dreams under your feet;
Tread softly because you tread on my dreams.

W B Yeats (1865 – 1939)

71 'Atelier 90' Group
Painted Calligraphy. Machine Embroidery. Bobbin and Machine Lace

72 Heather Ritchie
Rag Rug Hooking

He Wishes For
the Cloths of Heaven

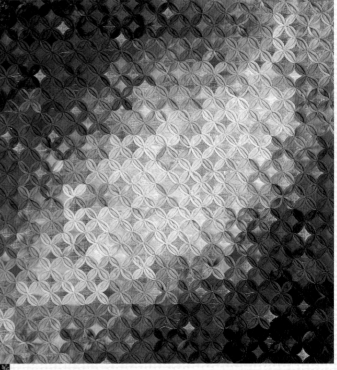

73 Margaret Dick
Cathedral Window Patchwork. Hand Stitched

74 Judith Anderson
Crazy Patchwork. Machine Stitched

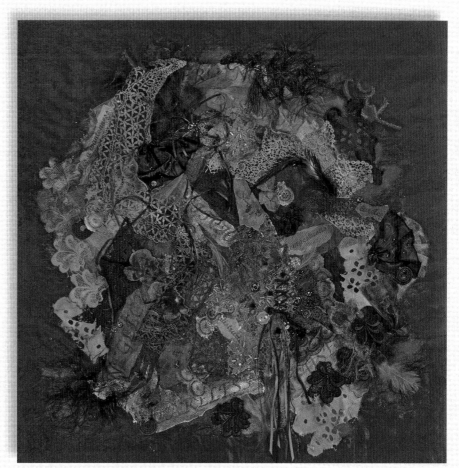

Delight in Disorder

A sweet disorder in the dress
Kindles in clothes a wantonness:
A lawn about the shoulders thrown
Into a fine distraction:
An erring lace which here and there
Enthrals the crimson stomacher:
A cuff neglectful, and thereby
Ribbons to flow confusedly:
A winning wave (deserving note)
In the tempestuous petticoat:
A careless shoe-string, in whose tie
I see a wild civility:
Do more bewitch me than when art
Is too precise in every part.

Robert Herrick (1591-1674)

75 Glynda Morrison
Free Machine Embroidery with Bead Embellishment

76 Marilyn Chaplin
Fabric Collage. Hand and Machine Embroidery

51

Leisure

WHAT is this life if, full of care,
We have no time to stand and stare?

No time to stand beneath the boughs,
And stare as long as sheep and cows:

No time to see, when woods we pass,
Where squirrels hide their nuts in grass:

No time to see, in broad daylight,
Streams full of stars, like skies at night:

No time to turn at Beauty's glance,
And watch her feet, how they can dance:

No time to wait till her mouth can
Enrich that smile her eyes began?

A poor life this if, full of care,
We have no time to stand and stare.

W. H. Davies (1871-1940)

77 Gillian Wright
Embellished Fabrics and Threads applied to Rug Canvas

78 Linda Connell
Applique with Machine Quilting

Harvest Time:
A Needlework Map

Our village holds no special place
In history. Its public face
Would cause no traveller to pause,
Its landscape merits no applause.

We love it though. And love declares
Its memories, in patchwork squares,
And fabric images that bind
The heritage we leave behind.
Each public, private, thought portrayed,
Each delicately appliquéd.

We stretch our memories on frames,
Without exaggerated claims,
Knowing each proud biography
Embroiders our geography.
This warning, too, our needles know,
That as we reap, so shall we sew.

Con Connell (1949 -   )

53

79 Malini Alagaratnam
Painted Fabric. Hand Embroidery

Trees

I think that I shall never see
A poem lovely as a tree.
A tree whose hungry mouth is prest
Against the sweet earth's flowing breast;
A tree that looks at God all day,
And lifts her leafy arms to pray;
A tree that may in summer wear
A nest of robins in her hair;
Upon whose bosom snow has lain;
Who intimately lives with rain.
Poems are made by fools like me,
But only God can make a tree.

Joyce Kilmer (1886 - 1918)

80 Isabell Bourke
Embellished Fabric with Machine Quilting

The Tiger

Tyger! Tyger! burning bright
In the forest of the night
What immortal hand or eye
Could frame thy fearful symmetry?

In what distant deeps or skies
Burnt the fire of thine eyes?
On what wings dare he aspire?
What the hand dare seize the fire?

And what shoulder, and what art,
Could twist the sinews of thy heart?
And when thy heart began to beat,
What dread hand? and what dread feet?

What the hammer? what the chain?
In what furnace was thy brain?
What the anvil? what dread grasp
Dare its deadly terrors clasp?

When the stars threw down their spears,
And watered heaven with their tears,
Did he smile his work to see?
Did he who made the lamb make thee?

Tyger! Tyger! burning bright
In the forests of the night,
What immortal hand or eye
Dare frame thy fearful symmetry?

William Blake (1757-1827)

81 Amanda Green
Painted Fabric. Applique

82 Beryl Leach
Hand Embroidery

Do not stand at my Grave and Weep

Do not stand at my grave and weep
I am not there; I do not sleep.
I am a thousand winds that blow,
I am the diamond glints on snow,
I am the sun on ripened grain,
I am the gentle autumn rain.
When you awaken in the morning's hush
I am the swift uplifting rush
Of quiet birds in circling flight.
I am the soft starlight at night.
Do not stand at my grave and cry,
I am not there; I did not die.

Anon

The Charge of the Light Brigade (extract)

Half a league, half a league,
Half a league onward,
All in the valley of Death
Rode the six hundred.
"Forward, the Light Brigade!
"Charge for the guns!" he said:
Into the valley of Death
Rode the six hundred.

"Forward, the Light Brigade!"
Was there a man dismay'd?
Not tho' the soldier knew
Someone had blunder'd:
Their's not to make reply,
Their's not to reason why,
Their's but to do and die:
Into the valley of Death
Rode the six hundred.

Alfred, Lord Tennyson (1809 – 1892)

83 Brenda Curry
Machine Embroidery

84 Mary Butt
Patchwork and Applique. Hand Quilting

Winter

When icicles hang by the wall
  And Dick the shepherd blows his nail
And Tom bears logs into the hall
  And milk comes frozen home in pail,
When blood is nipp'd and ways be foul,
  Then nightly sings the staring owl,
           Tu-who;
Tu whit, tu-who, a merry note,
While greasy Joan doth keel the pot.

When all aloud the wind doth blow
  And coughing drowns the parson's saw
And birds sit brooding in the snow
  And Marian's nose looks red and raw,
When roasted crabs hiss in the bowl,
  Then nightly sings the staring owl,
           Tu-who;
Tu whit, tu-who, a merry note,
While greasy Joan doth keel the pot.

William Shakespeare (1564-1616)

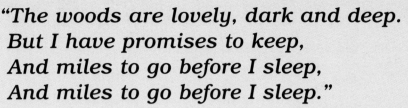

"The woods are lovely, dark and deep.
But I have promises to keep,
And miles to go before I sleep,
And miles to go before I sleep."

Robert Frost

Winter

Nature begins to tighten her grip once again, and the basic elements - fire, wind and water - are represented here. Winter is also a time for reflection, whether on the environment or on some personal contemplations of a more private, intimate world. And finally, the year ends with celebrations of mankind and Christmas.

The Highwayman (extract)

THE wind was a torrent of darkness among the gusty trees,
The moon was a ghostly galleon tossed upon cloudy seas,
The road was a ribbon of moonlight over the purple moor,
And the highwayman came riding—
          Riding—riding—
The highwayman came riding, up to the old inn-door.

He'd a French cocked-hat on his forehead, a bunch of lace at his chin,
A coat of the claret velvet, and breeches of brown doe-skin;
They fitted with never a wrinkle: his boots were up to the thigh!
And he rode with a jewelled twinkle,
          His pistol butts a-twinkle,
His rapier hilt a-twinkle, under the jewelled sky.

Over the cobbles he clattered and clashed in the dark inn-yard,
And he tapped with his whip on the shutters, but all was locked and barred;
He whistled a tune to the window, and who should be waiting there
But the landlord's black-eyed daughter,
          Bess, the landlord's daughter,
Plaiting a dark red love-knot into her long black hair.

Alfred Noyes (1880 – 1958)

85 Helen Judd
Patchwork and Applique

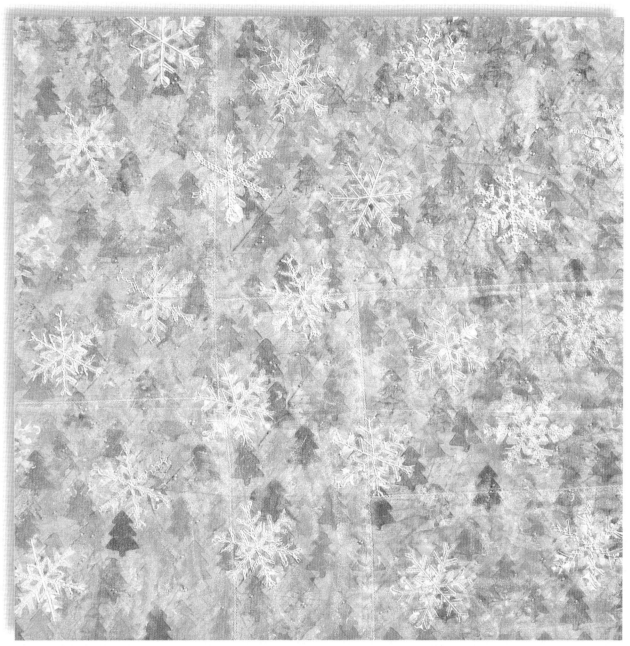

86 Karin Keddy
Painted Paper layered with Fabric. Hand Embroidery

Stopping By Woods On A Snowy Evening

Whose woods these are I think I know.
His house is in the village though;
He will not see me stopping here
To watch his woods fill up with snow.

My little horse must think it queer
To stop without a farmhouse near
Between the woods and frozen lake
The darkest evening of the year.

He gives his harness bells a shake
To ask if there is some mistake.
The only other sound's the sweep
Of easy wind and downy flake.

The woods are lovely, dark and deep.
But I have promises to keep,
And miles to go before I sleep,
And miles to go before I sleep.

Robert Frost (1874 – 1963)

Iona

Is this place really nearer to God?
Is the wall thin between our whispers
And his listening? I only know
The world grows less and less –
Here what matters is conquering the wind,
Coming home dryshod, getting the fire lit.
I'm not sure whether there is no time here
Or more time, whether the light is stronger
Or just easier to see. That is why
I keep returning, thirsty, to this place
That is older than my understanding,
Younger than my broken spirit.

Kenneth C Steven (1968 -   )

87 Anne Hough
Applique with Free Machine Embroidery

88 Deborah Smith
Machine Embroidery. Printing, Burning, Slashing & Bead Embellishment

Celtic Benediction

Deep peace of the running wave to you.
Deep peace of the flowing air to you.
Deep peace of the quiet earth to you.
Deep peace of the shining stars to you.
Deep peace of the son of peace to you.

J Philip Newell

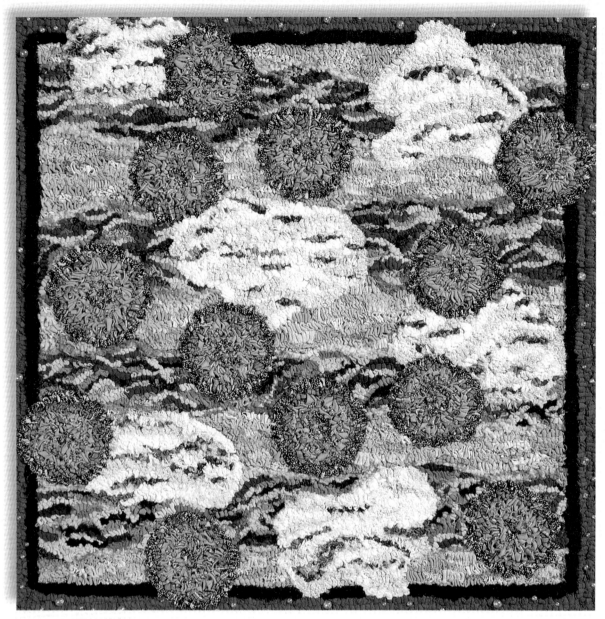

89 Helen McNicoll
Rag Rug Hooking

Thankfulness for Water

Raindrops fall silently
Like tears down a face
To swell God's life-giving drink
Held in puddle pond and river
Swirling out to oceans deep
Filling the font
At our heavenly beginning
Part of our whole being
Cleansing restoring and soothing
Rocked by storms
Evaporated by heat
Wasted by greed
Transformed into wine
Washing away sin
Feed on my lambs
There at our last washing
And for the disciples' feet
The blood of creation
Oh thank you our Father

Helen McNicoll (1942 -   )

Wind Farm

The great propellers idle
in the evening breeze,
as if the fields were just
preparing for departure
needing only favourable
alignment of the anticyclone
to give lift-off, into the teeth
of the Atlantic gale
raising the hillside, scattering
ploughed loam and trailing
filaments of light for all
the farms and villages around.

Tony Lucas (1941 -   )

90 Barbara West
Applique

91 Judith Anderson
Applique with Hand Stitching. Machine Quilted

92 Jenny Sweeney
Patchwork and Applique. Machine Quilting

Coal Fire

And once in some swamp forest, these
Were trees.
Before the first fox thought to run,
These dead black chips were one
Green net to hold the sun.
Each leaf in turn was taught the right
Way to drink light;
The twigs were made to learn
How to catch flame and yet not burn;
Branch and bough began to eat
Their diet of heat.
And so for years, six million years or higher,
They held that fire.

And here, out of the embers that remain,
That fire is loose again.
See how its hundred hands reach here and there,
Finger the air;
Then growing bolder, twisting free,
It fastens on the remnants of the tree
And, one by one,
Consumes them; mounts beyond them; leaps; is done;
And goes back to the sun.

Louis Untermeyer (1885 – 1977)

The Newcomer

'There's something new in the river,'
The fish said as it swam.
'It's got no scales, no fins and no gills,
And ignores the impassable dam.'

'There's something new in the trees.'
I heard a bloated thrush sing.
'It's got no beak, no claws, and no feathers,
And not even the ghost of a wing.'

'There's something new in the warren,'
Said the rabbit to the doe.
'It's got no fur, no eyes and no paws,
Yet digs further than we dare go.'

'There's something new in the whiteness,'
Said the snow-bright polar bear.
'I saw its shadow on a glacier,
But it left no pawmarks there.'

Through the animal kingdom
The news was spreading fast.
No beak, no claws, no feather,
No scales, no fur, no gills,
It lives in the trees and the water,
In the soil and the snow and the hills,
And it kills and it kills and it kills.

Brian Patten (1946 -   )

93 Judith Anderson
Mixed Materials, Machine Stitching

94 Judith Anderson
Dyed Fabric with Hand and Machine Embroidery

95 Melanie Philpott
Hand Embroidery

Tempo

I have a sense of future,
I feel naked in today,
  let me hurry into tomorrow
  it gives a promise of perhaps.
Let me escape these cloying yesterdays,
I sense a better perfume,
Let me wash away these footprints
I don't want people to know where
                 I've been
I want them to guess where I am.

Spike Milligan (1918 – 2002)

The Spoken Word

If I didn't have words
Then I couldn't offend
Couldn't say things to others
That I couldn't amend

Couldn't get into trouble
For something I said
Or get all embarrassed
And start turning red

To communicate with others
Verbal lines would be broken
Body language would take over
For no words would be spoken

Sometimes I think
No words would be good
Words can be overrated
And misunderstood

Edie Suarez (1960 -)

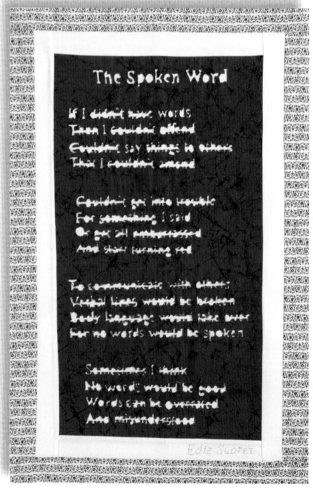

96 Rachel Wade
Cut work

97 Claire Fell
Image Transfer with Machine Embroidery

An Essay on Man (extract)

Know then thyself, presume not God to scan;
The proper study of mankind is man.
Placed on this isthmus of a middle state,
A being darkly wise, and rudely great:
With too much knowledge for the sceptic side,
With too much weakness for the stoic's pride,
He hangs between; in doubt to act, or rest;
In doubt to deem himself a god, or beast;
In doubt his mind or body to prefer;
Born but to die, and reasoning but to err;
Alike in ignorance, his reason such,
Whether he thinks too little, or too much:
Chaos of thought and passion, all confused;
Still by himself abused, or disabused;
Created half to rise, and half to fall;
Great lord of all things, yet a prey to all;
Sole judge of truth, in endless error hurled:
The glory, jest, and riddle of the world!

Alexander Pope (1688–1744)

98 Margaret Barraclough
Applique with Hand Embroidery

Abou Ben Adhem

Abou Ben Adhem (may his tribe increase!)
Awoke one night from a deep dream of peace,
And saw, within the moonlight in his room,
Making it rich, and like a lily in bloom,
An Angel writing in a book of gold:

Exceeding peace had made Ben Adhem bold,
And to the Presence in the room he said,
"What writest thou?" The Vision raised its head,
And with a look made of all sweet accord
Answered, "The names of those who love the Lord."

"And is mine one?" said Abou. "Nay, not so,"
Replied the Angel. Abou spoke more low,
But cheerily still; and said, "I pray thee, then,
Write me as one who loves his fellow men."

The Angel wrote, and vanished. The next night
It came again with a great wakening light,
And showed the names whom love of God had blessed,
And, lo! Ben Adhem's name led all the rest!

James Leigh Hunt (1784 – 1859)

Hymn on the morning of Christ's Nativity (verse 13)

Ring out ye Crystall sphears,
Once bless our human ears,
   (If ye have power to touch our senses so)
And let your silver chime
Move in melodious time;
   And let the Base of Heav'ns deep Organ blow
And with your ninefold harmony
Make up full consort to th'Angelike symphony.

John Milton (1608 – 1674)

99 Helen Allen
Layered Fabrics. Hand Embroidery

Samplers

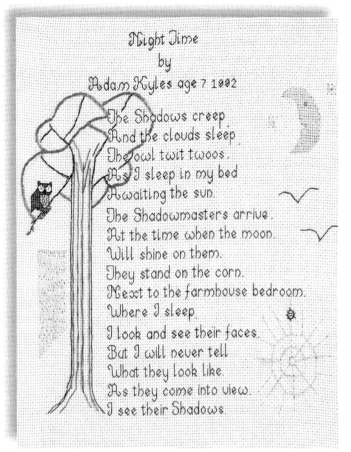

100 June Bower
Canvas Work

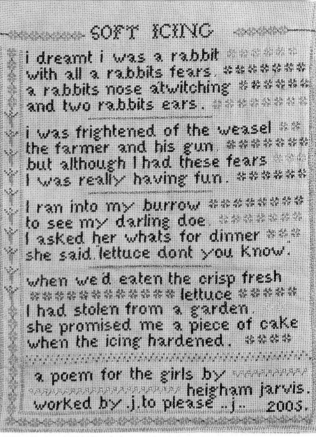

101 Jenny Jarvis
Canvas Work

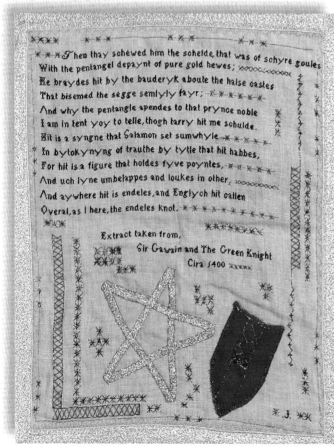

102 Jenny Jarvis
Canvas Work

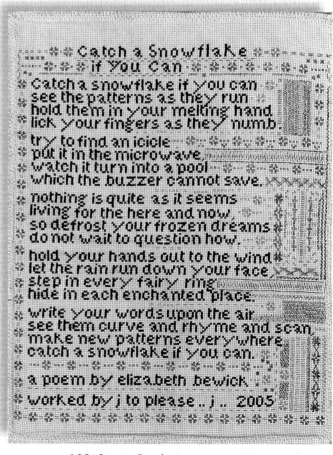

103 Jenny Jarvis
Canvas Work

Acknowledgements

The *National Needlework Archive* wishes to thank the following for permission to reprint copyright material.
Elizabeth Bewick 'Catch a Snowflake if You Can' from *Heartsease* ©Elizabeth Bewick 1991, reproduced by permission of Peterloo Poets. **Con Connell** 'Harvest Time' from *Essential Poems for Britain*, published by Harper Collins 2003 ©Con Connell 2003. 'Just One More' and 'Planetary Alignment' ©Con Connell 2004, reprinted by permission of the author. **Wendy Cope** 'Traditional Prize County Pigs: Staffordshire Tamworth Red' from *If I Don't Know* published by Faber and Faber ©Wendy Cope 2001, reprinted by permission of the author. **W.H. Davies** 'Leisure' from *The Oxford Book of English Verse*, published by OUP 1939. Reprinted by permission of Dee & Griffin, Trustees for the Estate of W.H. Davies. **Alec Finlay** 'Circle Poem', ©Alec Finlay 2004, printed by permission of the author. **Robert Frost** 'Stopping by Woods on a Snowy Evening' from *The Poetry of Robert Frost* edited by Edward Connery Latham. Copyright 1923, 1969 by Henry Holt and Company, copyright 1951 by Robert Frost. Reprinted by permission of Henry Holt and Company LLC. **Mike Harding** 'The Green Man' reprinted by permission of the author. **M. Louise Haskins** 'The Gate of the Year' from *Poetry Please* published by Phoenix Poetry 2002 ©M. Louise Haskins 1908, reprinted by permission of Sheil Land Associates. **Antonio Carlos Jobim** 'Waters of March' ©Antonio Carlos Jobim, used by permission of Corcovado Music Corporation, Mineola, NY. **Jenny Joseph** 'Warning' from *Selected Poems*, published by Bloodaxe Books, 1992 ©Jenny Joseph 1992, reprinted by permission of the author. **Dorothea MacKellar** 'My Country' from *Convict Creations* published by Wally De Villiers ©Dorothea MacKellar, reprinted by permission of Curtis Brown (Aus) Pty Ltd on behalf of the Estate of Dorothea MacKellar. **John Masefield** 'Sea Fever' reprinted by permission of the Society of Authors as the Literary Representative of the Estate of John Masefield. **Helen McNicoll** 'Thankfulness for Water' from *The Poetry Church*, published by Feather Books ©Helen McNicoll 2001, reprinted by permission of the author. **Spike Milligan** 'Tempo' from *The Mirror Running* published by Michael Joseph ©Spike Milligan 1987. Reprinted by permission of Spike Milligan Productions Ltd. **Mike Mockler** 'Redstart in a Welsh Wood' from *Flights of Imagination*, Blandford Press 1982 ©Mike Mockler 1982, reprinted by permission of the author. **J. Philip Newell** 'Celtic Benediction' ©J. Philip Newell 2000, reprinted by permission of the author. **Alfred Noyes** 'The Highwayman', reprinted by permission of the Society of Authors as the Literary Representative of the Estate of Alfred Noyes. **Mary Oliver** 'Wild Geese' from *Dream Work* published by Atlantic Monthly Press Inc 1986 © Mary Oliver 1986, reprinted by permission of Grove/Atlantic Inc. **Henry Reed** 'Naming of Parts' from *Lessons of the War*, reprinted by permission of John Tyderman and The Royal Literary Fund. **Osbert Sitwell** 'Mrs Southern's Enemy' from *Collected Poems of Osbert Sitwell* published by Duckworth and Co Ltd, 1931, reprinted by permission of David Higham Associates. **Kenneth C. Steven** 'Iona' from *Iona: Poems*, published by Saint Andrews Press 2000 ©Kenneth C. Steven 2000, reprinted by permission of the author. **Richard Stewart** 'After Dark at Yachtsman's Cottage' from *Remembrance* published by Hilton House Books 1999 ©Richard Stewart 1999. 'Nocturne' from *Green Man*, published by Poetry Monthly Press 2004 ©Richard Stewart 2004, reprinted by permission of the author. **Louis Untermeyer** 'Coal Fire' from *The Golden Treasury of Poetry* published by W Collins & Co Ltd, 1961. Permission is granted by arrangement with the Estate of Louis Untermeyer, Norma Anchin Untermeyer c/o Professional Publishing Services. The reprint is granted with the expressed permission by Laurence S. Untermeyer. **W.B. Yeats** 'He wishes for the Cloths of Heaven' from *The Collected Poems of W.B. Yeats*, reprinted by permission of A.P. Watt Ltd on behalf of Michael B. Yeats.

We are grateful to the following, whose work was previously published in *Poems In The Waiting Room*, for permission to reprint their work here. **Tony Lucas** 'Wind Farm', ©Tony Lucas 2003, reprinted by permission of the author. **Edie Suarez** 'The Spoken Word' ©Edie Suarez 2002, reprinted by permission of the author. **Maggie Butt** 'Bulbs', ©Maggie Butt, reprinted by permission of the author. **Stewart Conn** 'Cherry Tree at Dusk', from *Stolen Light* published by Bloodaxe Books 1999, ©Stewart Conn 1999, reprinted by permission of the author. **Helen Clare** 'Marigolds' from *Magma* Autumn 2000 ©Helen Clare 2000, reprinted by permission of the author. **J.R. Prynne** 'Chill' ©J.R. Prynne 2000, reprinted by permission of the Estate of J.R Prynne. **Dee Rimbaud** 'Dream Eclipses Reality' from *The Bad Seed*, published by Stride, 1998 ©Dee Rimbaud 1998, reprinted by permission of the author. **Tony Turner** 'Fast Bowler' ©Tony Turner 2003, reprinted by permission of the author. **Mollie Mayson** 'Hawk in the grey Morning' ©Mollie Mayson 2002, reprinted by permission of the author. **Idris Caffrey** 'The Other Side of the Valley' ©Idris Caffrey reprinted by permission of the author. **Rainer Maria Rilke** 'Sunset', translation copyright ©Michael Lee 2005. **Peter Williamson** 'Streetwonders' ©Peter Williamson. This poem was first published in the *New York Times* and appeared subsequently in *Footholds: Selected Poems 1976 – 1996* (Brentham Press). Reprinted by permission of the author. **Joan Kingston** 'Questions in Eden' ©Joan Kingston 2004, reprinted by permission of the author. **Pippa Hardy** 'Rainbow' ©Pippa Hardy 2003, reprinted by permission of the author. **Isobel M. Campbell** 'Millstone Quarry' ©Isobel M. Campbell 1999, reprinted by permission of the author. **Joan Goodall** 'I would not have you perfect' ©Joan Goodall 2000, reprinted by permission of the author. **Jose Segal** 'Ivy' ©Jose Segal 2004, reprinted by permission of the author.

We are also grateful to the following authors, whose work is published here for the first time. **Dawn M. Ashcroft** 'Sound of Song' ©Dawn Ashcroft 2005, reprinted by permission of the author. **Rebecca Atherton** 'Stitched Together Over Time' ©Rebecca Atherton 2004, reprinted by permission of the author. **Delia Garrod** 'Empty' ©Delia Garrod 1977, reprinted by permission of the author. **Adam Kyles** 'Night Time' ©Adam Kyles 1992, reprinted by permission of the author. **Doreen E. Davis** 'The Long Awaited Snowdrop' ©Doreen E. Davis 1986, reprinted by permission of the author. **Heigham Jarvis** 'Soft Icing' ©Heigham Jarvis 1968, reprinted by permission of the author. **Ina K. Leavers** 'Partings' ©I.K. Leavers 2002, reprinted by permission of Mrs P Duerden on behalf of the Estate of I.K. Leavers. **Prue FitzGerald** 'Red Gleam' ©Prue FitzGerald reprinted by permission of the author.

The publishers have made every effort to trace copyright holders of material reproduced within this compilation. The publishers apologize if any material has been included without permission or without appropriate acknowledgement, and would be glad to correct any oversights or errors in future editions.

Tips and Troubleshooting for Good Finishing and Presentation of Textile Pictures

Wall-hangings and pictures for exhibitions or other public displays have to look good, and be stable, strong, and secure. The appearance of work to be displayed in your own home, or to be given to friends, will also be greatly enhanced by good presentation methods.

It is essential that you take time and care with the finish and presentation of your work. After spending hours, weeks or months working on your picture, it deserves to be well finished in order to show it off to its best advantage. Well presented work looks fabulous while a poorly presented piece will never look really good, however brilliant the imagery, stitching, or technique. It is also true that a piece that maybe didn't work out quite as well as expected can be greatly improved by good finishing techniques.

The size of Poetry in Stitches pictures is 61cm x 61cm (24" x 24") square, but most of the following tips will be equally useful for work of other shapes and sizes. These notes cover the most straightforward and easiest of finishes to give you a good result.

The method of finishing which is the most suitable for your individual work will be determined by several factors, including the techniques used to create the picture, the method of construction, the thickness of the completed work, and the desired effect. Choose the method that you feel is most appropriate to give your work a robust finish and excellent appearance.

During the actual making of the piece, try to ensure you are keeping the work to the planned size and shape by regularly checking its progress. This will give you the opportunity to address any major problems as soon as they become apparent, and before they are so far back in the making process that they cannot be absorbed or recovered.

When the picture is finished lay it down and check for parallel edges, square corners, and, if it is supposed to be flat, for an even and flat surface.

Work is rarely perfect at this point so don't panic! There is a lot that can be done to help bring problems into line.

Embroideries

Embroideries can be presented as soft hangings; laced over mounting boards; or stretched and stapled to sub-frames. But first the work needs to be properly finished by tying off all loose ends, pressing or blocking, and straightening the edges.

Finishing

Some embroideries only need to be lightly pressed before mounting, to straighten the grain and remove slight creasing.

Pressing Method:

Place the work face down on a dry towel. Lightly spray with water or use a dampened pressing cloth and apply light pressure to the back. Remember, pressing is not ironing. Pressing is putting the iron down on the fabric with the appropriate pressure for that fabric, usually using a pressing cloth, and then lifting it straight up, before placing it down again further over. Pressing should not distort the fabric but, especially if using moisture to create steam, pressing should fix the fabric in the required shape or direction. Pressed-in creases are difficult to remove so embroideries should only be lightly pressed from the wrong side, being careful that you are achieving the desired effect, and are not flattening the surface threads.

After pressing, leave the embroidery in place until quite dry.

If pressing is sufficient to remove creases and puckering, and to generally firm up your work, then proceed to straighten the edges. Your work is going to be easier to mount if the edges are straight.

Edges should be trimmed straight with a ruler and rotary cutter. Check the sides, and top and bottom edges are equal in length. Check the corners of the work are right angled by ensuring the diagonal measurements from corner to corner across the face of the work are equal [Fig.1].

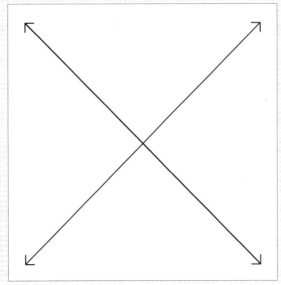

Fig. 1

Many embroideries, and all canvas work, will benefit from being stretched, or 'blocked' before mounting or framing. This technique will straighten up even badly distorted grain lines and will bring misshapen work back from the brink. It is well worth the trouble.

Blocking Method:

1. Take a piece of flat board that it is possible to stick pins in (e.g. thick polystyrene or fibreboard), and which is slightly bigger than the embroidery. First cover the board with a piece of polythene to prevent possible staining from the board, and then cover it with a towel. If you have selvedge edges on the embroidery or canvas, snip through the selvedge several times along its length to avoid puckering. Lay the embroidery face down on the towel and, starting in the middle of each of the four sides, carefully pull the sides out taut so they are straight and square, straightening the grain, and pinning as you go out towards the corners – working on all sides evenly at the same time. The pins go in at an angle through the edges of the fabric into the board beneath (Fig.2).

When the work is fully pinned out, lightly dampen by spraying the back with water and then leave to dry naturally. Do not try to over-stretch the fabric in one go. Do a little at a time and re-block in this way several times if this is necessary.

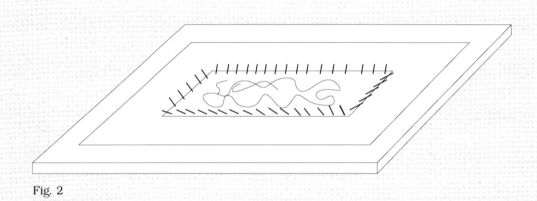

Fig. 2

2. If there is a lot of surface texture, or raised work, on the embroidery that could be flattened by the above method, then use this alternative. Take the same board, cover it with polythene and then with white blotting paper. Lightly dampen the blotting paper all over with water. Lay the embroidery face up on the blotting paper and pin out as before. Leave to dry naturally. In both cases it is the back of the work which is in contact with the moisture, not the front.

(It is best to use de-ionised water which is available from most large chemists. This will greatly reduce the occurrence of those tiny 'rust' looking marks that can appear on old fabrics)

Presentation

The majority of embroideries need to be permanently mounted on a support to give a good presentation to the embroidery and to enhance the appearance of the thread work. There are two basic methods of mounting:

Mounting and Lacing over a Board: Take a piece of acid free mounting board cut to the required finished size of the picture. The board should be in one piece, and substantial enough not to bend when the textile picture is stretched over it. Position the picture as desired, face outwards, onto the front of the board and fold the raw edges of the top and bottom over to the back of the board, leaving the two side edges free.

(Ideally, there should be at least 7.5cms (3") of fabric available to turn over to the back on all four sides for a picture sized 61cms x 61cms (24" x 24"). If one or more sides have less than this, extend the edge by machine stitching an extra strip of fabric along the short edge. Working with deep and even turnbacks is much easier than trying to lace uneven or scimpy edges, and gives a much neater finish.)

Lay the board and picture face downwards and, starting in the middle and working out towards the edge, lace the two turned-over edges together across the back of the picture using a large needle and strong thread (Fig.3).

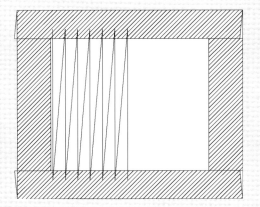

Fig. 3

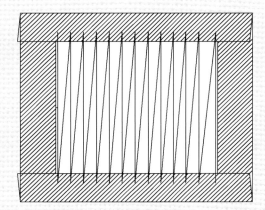

Fig. 4

Re-check the correct positioning of the picture front and then finish lacing the other half of the back (Fig.4). Repeat this procedure with the two side edges, laying the new laces over the laced threads already in position (Fig.5). Neatly hand finish the corners. This method gives a taut and sturdy presentation and is easy to work. It is very effective when used with a layer of thin wadding to cover the board underneath the embroidery if a softer finish, or more relief, is required. For a really tidy finish the back should be covered with a board or lining cloth.

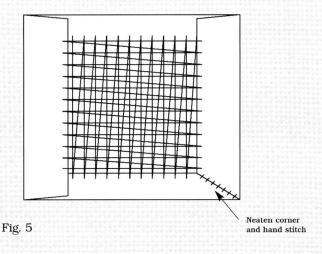

Fig. 5

Neaten corner
and hand stitch

Mounting on a frame: Some embroideries (especially larger pieces of work), are best mounted on a wooden sub-frame. This is a simple wooden square of timber, fixed together at the corners. The fabric around the edge of the embroidery must be sufficient to turn right over to the back of the sub-frame, and the sub-frame must be substantial enough not to twist when under tension. For large pieces of work the sub-frame should be reinforced with cross pieces.

Position the embroidery as desired over the front of the frame and turn all the edges over to the back. Lay the work and the frame down on its face and, starting in the middle of all four sides, fix the fabric edges in position on the back of the frame with drawing pins. Working all sides at the same time, pin out the edges towards the corners of the frame, keeping the embroidery taut, but not overstretched. When this is completed, and the picture finally checked for correct positioning on the front, gradually replace the drawing pins by fixing with rust resistant tacks or staples. Turn in the loose corners of the work neatly and tack or staple in position. (Fig.6)

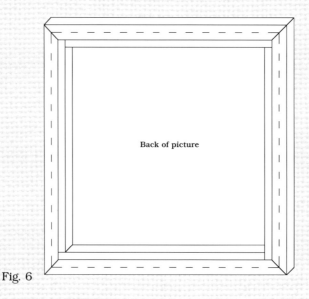

Back of picture

Fig. 6

Either mounting method is suitable for display, or for further decorative framing. Poetry in Stitches pieces should be left without decorative frames.

Soft Embroidered Hangings

Soft embroidered hangings benefit from being interfaced and lined to help give them body and maintain their shape.

Facing and Lining Method: The weight of the interfacing will depend on the hanging but should be sufficiently heavy to allow the edges of the embroidery to be turned over to the back of the interfacing and stitched down without making the edges curl. A herringbone stitch is best for this and these retaining stitches should not go through to the front fabric. A lining fabric can then be attached to the back and slip stitched to the turned edges of the work (Fig.7).

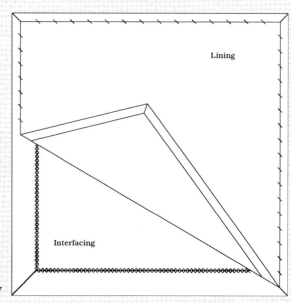

Lining

Interfacing

Fig. 7

Quilts

Quilts generally have an improved appearance if they lie flat and have even, neat edges. Most quilt instruction books give details of construction techniques and binding methods but here are a few tips for those quilts that, even after all your care, still turn out lumpy or irregular!

Before you put the final binding on, lay the quilt down and assess its appearance.

Are the edges parallel?

If your quilt is to be hung up and displayed, then parallel edges are important. If the quilt is narrower across the top than across the bottom, or one side is longer than the other, it would be best to try and stretch the short edge and ease in the longer edge, to get parallel edges of the same length without too much effect on the main body of the quilt. This can be done by cutting the binding for the unequal edges to an equal length. Mark the required length of the finished edge on to the two bindings, and when you pin it to the quilt, gently stretch the short edge of the quilt to fit between these marks, and ease in the excess on the longer edge of the quilt. This will not work for edges with a difference in length of more than about 5cms (2").

Example -   *The length of the binding required for the two edges can be worked out as follows:*
For two unequal side lengths of 58" and 60" (ie 2" difference)

Add together: *An allowance for the corner treatment at one end (eg 4")*
+ The length of the shorter edge plus half the difference in the side lengths (eg 58"+1"= 59")
+ an allowance for the corner treatment at other end (eg 4")
= The length of the binding (eg 4" + 59" + 4" = 67")

Are the edges straight?

Even though you will have made sure the quilt top was straight and square before you attached the wadding and backing sandwich, once the quilting is finished the quilt may have distorted. Follow the instructions below for blocking the quilt to pull it into shape.

However, if the edges are really uneven and blocking doesn't help, it may be better to cut them straight and then attach a wider, padded binding to bring the picture up to the desired size, than to bind bad edges that will never look straight. The suitability of this method will depend on your design.

Does your quilt lie flat?

Quilts which have been very closely quilted are particularly prone to looking lumpy when completed. This is often due to the tension of the stitching being too tight or uneven. This can be helped during making by using a hoop or frame. Gently blocking a finished quilt can improve a lumpy appearance and can also help to pull it into shape and square. Quilts should not be pressed.

Does your quilt picture have good right angled corners?

If not, it will look very disappointing when hung. This fault can also be improved by blocking, and by careful application of the binding.

The method for blocking a quilt is very similar to that for blocking a piece of embroidery (see page 76). The difference is that you will be pinning to the board with the quilt face upwards and then lightly spraying the right side face of the work, not the reverse side.

You will be trying to obtain straight, even, sides and square corners, so gently stretch out sides which are too short, at the same time as gently easing-in sides which are too long. Do this as you are pinning out the quilt so that corresponding sides are pinned to the same length. (If doing this with a large quilt, a fitted carpet covered with a blanket is an ideal 'pinning board'). When pinned out, re-check the measurements top to bottom and side to side, and diagonally across the corners. Very lightly spray the quilt with water and leave to dry naturally before removing the pins. This method can be repeated several times until you are satisfied with the result.

Rugs

Rugs need to be square and to lie flat. Extra rows of fabric can be hooked into the edges to straighten them. Any excess hessian around the edges of the rug can be turned to the back and stitched into place as a binding. Alternatively, bind with an appropriate fabric such as wide twill tape. The binding tape should be stitched as close as possible to the outer rows of hooking, and can be stitched by hand or machine (Fig 8). Start attaching the binding in the middle of a side, and leave enough fullness in the binding at the corners to allow for turning the binding to the back of the rug. Finish attaching the binding with a slanted seam at the join and hem stitch the loose edge of the binding to the back of the rug (Fig 9).

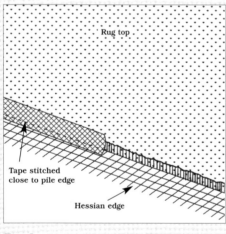

Fig. 8

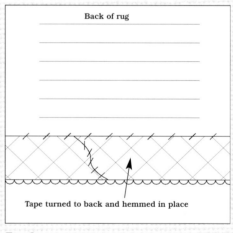

Fig. 9

Rugs can be pressed to give a flat and even finish. Lay the rug face down on a towel and cover the wrong side with a damp pressing cloth. Using a hot iron, apply pressure evenly over the rug. Do not use a smoothing, ironing motion. Leave the rug in position until completely dry. This can also be done to the front of the rug if you want a flatter finish to the upper surface.

All of these finishing techniques are well within the range of beginners, as well as experienced stitchers and craftworkers. If you have taken the trouble to make a lovely piece of work, then finish and present it to the best of your ability. The work will last much longer, and will be a source of pride for you, and of admiration and interest to others.

Index

Pictures are numbered from No.1 at the beginning of the book, through to No. 103 at the end, in numerical order.